# DAILY PRAYER PROJECT

ANIMATING A LIFE OF PRAYER THROUGH THE MANIFOLD BEAUTY OF THE CHURCH

# Credits

Unless otherwise indicated, scripture quotations are taken from The Holy Bible, English Standard Version®.Copyright ©2001 by Crossway Bibles, a division of GoodNews Publishers. Used by permission. All rights reserved.

*Canyon Road: A Book of Prayer* by Kari Kristina Reeves. ©2016 Atlas Spiritual Designs. This beautiful and highly recommended volume can be purchased at www.exploreatlas.com. Used by permission.

*I Lie on My Mat and Pray: Prayers by Young Africans*, edited by Fritz Pawelzik. ©1964 Friendship Press.

*Morning, Noon and Night: Prayers and Meditations Mainly from the Third World*, collected and introduced by John Carden. ©1976 Church Missionary Society, London.

*Oceans of Prayer,* compiled by Maureen Edwards and Jan S. Pickard. ©1991 National Christian Education Council.

*The Oxford Book of Prayer,* edited by George Appleton. ©2002 Oxford University Press.

*Prayers Ancient and Modern*, selected by Mary Wilder Tileston (New York: Grosset & Dunlap, 1897). PublicDomain.

*Seeing Christ in Others: An Anthology for Worship, Meditation and Mission*, compiled and edited by Geoffrey Duncan. ©1998 United Church Publishing House, Toronto, Canada.

## Staff & Contributors

CO-DIRECTOR
Joel Littlepage

CO-DIRECTOR
Ashley Williams

EDITOR
Russ Whitfield

CURATOR
& COPYEDITOR
Victoria Emily Jones

DESIGNER
Lauren Hofer
Atlas Minor Design Studio

If you would like to receive rights to print and distribute this volume to an organization or congregation, please contact us at team@dailyprayerproject.com to discuss our subscription plan.

The Daily Prayer Project is produced as a ministry of Grace Mosaic in Northeast Washington, DC.

Grace Mosaic is a congregation of the Grace DC Network.

# TABLE OF CONTENTS

*Erik Gazi*

# LETTER FROM THE DIRECTOR

JOEL LITTLEPAGE

To be welcomed is the deep yearning of every human heart; to be shunned, its greatest fear. The Christian movement, in whatever place and amid whatever cultures it finds itself, is always struggling between "exclusion and embrace," as the Croatian theologian Miroslav Volf famously explores in his book of the same title. Volf writes of the tragedy of exclusion when the people who claim the name of the Triune God practice a "kind of purity that wants the world cleansed of the other rather than the heart cleansed of the evil that drives people out by calling those who are clean 'unclean' and refusing to help make clean those who are unclean."

Pentecost is the great welcome of the Creator to all nations and peoples. The outpouring of the Holy Spirit was strikingly and disturbingly indiscriminate for those ethnically or culturally Jewish Christians witnessing it in those early days of the Way. It took divine intervention to move Peter to his cross-cultural conversion moment when he finally got it after watching Cornelius, a Gentile Roman man, be welcomed by God: "Truly I understand that God shows no partiality, but in every nation anyone who fears him and does what is right is acceptable to him" (Acts 10:34–35). The phrase "no partiality" refers, linguistically, to God's disposition to "lift the face" of anyone who bows down toward his presence, thereby experiencing the radical embrace of God. The move of Pentecost is, fundamentally, a movement from exclusion to embrace. The Spirit always leads the way. Our work at the Daily Prayer Project is the work of welcome. We seek to animate the life of prayer through the manifold beauty of the church. That is fundamentally practiced through a posture of hospitable welcome: recognizing the manifold gifts of the Spirit within the people of God of every time and place and receiving their outpourings of prayers, art, practice, and song as treasured gifts. Our prayer is that every day of prayer would fill us all with continual wonder that we have been brought into something so much larger than ourselves: the new creation of the Spirit, the beautiful mosaic of God's people from every tribe, tongue, and nation from generation to generation. Praise be to the God who fills "all in all" (Eph. 1:23).

We celebrate and join in prayer with a vastly diverse church in this edition of the DPP. The American artist Carol Aust's 2015 painting *Breaking Bread* displays the quintessential image of the welcome of the Lord and his body: the table. The church of Latin America gifts us with the traditional corito (praise song) "No hay dios tan grande como tú," which includes the lines *No es con espada, ni con ejércitos, mas con su Santo Espíritu* ("Not by our weapons, nor by our power, but by your Spirit we are led"). The former queen of Tonga, Sālote Tupou III, prays, "We are different from one another in race and language, in material things, in gifts, in opportunities, but each of us has a human heart, knowing joy and sorrow, pleasure and pain. We are one in our need of your forgiveness, your strength, your love." Finally, in the Practices, the Rev. Dr. Abe Cho, exploring feasting and the spiritual significance of meals, suggests that if beauty is compelled to make copies of itself, then the sacramental table of the Lord's Supper compels each of us to consider that "if I am formed by this meal with Jesus, . . . then at every table I sit, I am to take with me the practices of reconciliation, the practices of forgiveness, and the practices of the kingdom."

This time of Pentecost that we celebrate together is a global feast in which we rejoice in the variety of gifts and graces the Spirit has given to the people of God. We pray that the manifold beauty of the church would shine powerfully through every page of this edition and lead you, by the Spirit, to the fountain of all beauty: the Father, the Son, and the Holy Spirit. Amen, amen, and amen.

# INTRODUCTION

The Daily Prayer Project (DPP) is a movement that exists to animate the life of prayer through the manifold beauty of the church. We connect and unify Christians by resourcing them with daily prayers, practices, and music from the global-historical church, and visual art of spiritual and artistic value. All of these rich resources are crafted into a simple, functional, and beautiful product: our Living Prayer Periodicals (LPPs). This is what you are holding in your hands right now.

We produce six LPP editions per year that move with the Christian seasons of Advent, Christmas & Epiphany, Lent, Easter, Pentecost, and Ordinary Time. These editions combine dynamic and diverse content with a stable method for morning and evening prayer.

This method not only provides consistency for the life of prayer and practice, but it also forms us all into a life of communion with God and unity with our global and historical family of faith. It is this communal prayer that fuels and forms our own expressions of prayer in the present season of our lives. The DPP is an entrance into the holy, unifying, and empowering experience of praying together in a common way without ceasing throughout the Christian year.

The Daily Prayer Project logo is a monogram crafted into a prayer labyrinth. The mark itself becomes a practice of prayer. Rooted in the ancient Christian tradition of pilgrimage, prayer labyrinths have a history as far back as the fourth century in an Algerian church.

A labyrinth is not a maze. There is one entry point, and a single pathway leading to the center. The journey is a transformative walk toward God, the center of the labyrinth. Arriving at the center symbolizes union with God. Once a pilgrim has this encounter, they are led back out into the world along the same path.

Walking a labyrinth is a slow, meditative practice. This is a way to embody your prayer. The mark is placed above for you to travel the path of the labyrinth with your finger as a small gesture of this larger practice. We hope that one day you might be able to encounter God as you walk through a physical prayer labyrinth.

# Daily Prayer Project Lectionary

A lectionary is a schedule of Bible readings that is meant to help Christians read the whole Bible over a period of time, emphasizing particular themes and narratives during particular seasons of the Christian year. The Daily Prayer Project follows the Sunday (and certain holy day) readings of the Revised Common Lectionary, the largest shared Bible-reading plan in North America. For most Monday–Saturdays, we follow our own Daily Prayer Project Lectionary, which moves through scripture in a slow, three-year cycle. The DPP Lectionary is broken down into three categories of readings from scripture: the Psalms, the Old Testament, and the New Testament. The Old Testament is broken down into its traditional three parts: (1) Law & History, (2) Wisdom & Poetic Literature, and (3) the Prophets. The New Testament is also broken down into its traditional three sections: (1) the Four Gospels & Acts, (2) the Pauline Epistles, and (3) the General Epistles. Lectionaries are a time-tested tool from the history of the church for maintaining a steady "diet" from the Bible's different parts. They are specifically designed to lighten the daily load of reading and to help the reader focus in on smaller passages and particular books at a time. This facilitates slower, more meditative reading. Currently, the DPP is in Year B of the lectionary.

| | YEAR A | YEAR B | YEAR C |
|---|---|---|---|
| **The Psalms** | ALL 150 PSALMS<br>2x/Year | ALL 150 PSALMS<br>2x/Year | ALL 150 PSALMS<br>2x/Year |
| **Old Testament** | LAW & HISTORY<br>Genesis–Leviticus<br><br>WISDOM & POETRY<br>Proverbs & Job<br><br>PROPHETS<br>Isaiah<br>& Minor Prophets (Part I) | LAW & HISTORY<br>Numbers–2 Samuel<br><br>WISDOM & POETRY<br>Proverbs & Ecclesiastes<br><br>PROPHETS<br>Jeremiah, Lamentations<br>& Minor Prophets (Part II) | LAW & HISTORY<br>1 Kings–Esther<br><br>WISDOM & POETRY<br>Proverbs & Song of Songs<br><br>PROPHETS<br>Ezekiel<br>& Minor Prophets (Part III) |
| **New Testament** | GOSPEL & ACTS<br>Matthew, Mark & Acts<br><br>PAULINE EPISTLES<br>Romans–Titus<br><br>GENERAL EPISTLES<br>Hebrews–Revelation | GOSPEL & ACTS<br>Luke & Acts<br><br>PAULINE EPISTLES<br>Romans–Titus<br><br>GENERAL EPISTLES<br>Hebrews–Revelation | GOSPEL & ACTS<br>John & Acts<br><br>PAULINE EPISTLES<br>Romans–Titus<br><br>GENERAL EPISTLES<br>Hebrews–Revelation |

*Sundays and holy days are from the Revised Common Lectionary*

# Methods & Elements

Each day of the LPP features morning and evening prayer liturgies framed by seven core elements. Everyone's style of praying is different because every person is different. Beyond that, Christian prayer varies widely across cultures and denominations. No single method can capture this. However, we hope you find within the LPP a rhythm that gives enough structure and freedom to facilitate a diverse community of prayer. Every element is offered as a guiding movement, not as a binding rule. You are encouraged to modify the liturgy based on the context of prayer. Consider establishing rhythms of prayer in your congregation, household, workplace, small groups, or other gatherings so that you might experience the formative reality of common prayer. If doing this liturgy individually, you are encouraged to take your time to soak it in. If doing it as a group, it may be best to alternate leading each element. Also, consider using different postures in prayer (standing, kneeling, lifted or open hands, lying prostrate, etc.) that fit your context.

CALL: There is an invitation always open to us. The Spirit of God calls us to come into the holy presence, and we respond to this welcome by entering in.

PSALM: The Psalms form the core language of prayer for the people of God and have done so for thousands of years. The Psalms give us language and postures of heart and body to express in the presence of God.

ADORATION: We were created to adore God, and in the place of worship we find the joy of this purpose. This adoration happens in both silence and song. We provide three to four songs per edition in the Songbook at the back. Full recordings and resources for these songs and others can be found at dailyprayerproject.com. You are also encouraged to sing songs from your own community.

LESSON: The scriptures give us the story of the Father's redemption of all things in the Son by the power of the Holy Spirit.

PRAYER: We are led across praise, confession, and guided intercessory prayer by our family of faith all over the globe and throughout time. We receive every prayer as a gift as we put them on our own lips and in our own hearts. These prayers range from traditional prayers of the universal church to more modern and meditative prayers.

ABIDING: In response to what we have encountered in the first five elements, Abiding is an opportunity for deeper communion and self-reflection through meditating on the scriptures (*lectio divina*), considering the art in the gallery (*visio divina*), or using our bodies to engage historical Christian practices (*praxio divina*). Out of that place, we are also prompted to pray for the needs of others in different stations of life.

BENEDICTION: We close our time with a word of love and blessing over our lives from God himself, the Alpha and the Omega, the Beginning and the End. Our journey of prayer is framed by the Call and the Benediction; God has the first and the last word over all things in our lives.

Nathan Dumlao

## Adapting the LPP for Household Prayer

*A Five-Element Method*

We have often been asked how to adapt the Living Prayer Periodicals for household prayer, especially when that involves small children. It is an important question and one for which we want to provide some suggestions. These suggestions come after years of practice and experimenting within our own communities and families. The liturgies can be practiced once or twice a day, depending on your household rhythms. In my house, we practice communal prayer around the table once we finish dinner (almost!) every evening.

Disclaimer: If you have small children, prayer time will probably not always be peaceful and beautiful. These times might involve some chaos, disordered noise, fighting, arguing, silly laughter, etc. That's OK! Especially as children begin developing new habits and growing in their ability to pay attention, you are encouraged to let them grow in this way and to take your time growing in prayer together. There is no hurry, and things need not be perfect. The Lord is with you and your family and merely desires your presence. The important part is finding a simple rhythm and sticking to it because children (and adults) thrive on rhythms.

The following suggested method takes the seven core elements of the LPP liturgies and reduces them to five:

**CALL**
**LESSON** (Psalm, OT, or NT)
**ABIDING**
**THE LORD'S PRAYER**
**BENEDICTION**

Here are some practical suggestions for implementing this method:

- Before you begin to pray together, select what your Lesson reading is going to be. For example, if the scripture readings that day are Psalm 62, Leviticus 12, and Mark 10, then choose one or a section of one of those to attend to. It will probably be best for those with small children to begin small. If Mark 10 is chosen, then choose just one of the sections of that chapter.
- Before you begin to pray together, distribute the parts of the liturgy to different members of the household. In my household we have five people, so each member is responsible for one movement of the liturgy. If you have children who can read, they might relish the chance to read a different part each day. We keep a chart on the wall with the day, the five elements, and the person's name, giving each person a chance to do different parts throughout the week.
- If children cannot read, worry not! Children also love to do call-and-response, and this is how their language is formed. For my youngest son, who cannot read, his mother or I whisper the words of the call in his ear and he then gets to say them loudly for the family prayer time. He loves it, and yes, it is often adorable.
- Begin each time of prayer by taking some breaths together as a family (we often do three deep breaths), bringing stillness to your bodies, hearts, and minds.
- CALL: Again, children often love call-and-response! If necessary, teach them what their response line is going to be (the words in bold). Then someone should read the call and hear the response of the rest of the table.
- LESSON: Read the passage of scripture you selected before, or have one of the children read it (mine fight over this privilege . . .).
- ABIDING: This element can be really flexible as far as what is done and how long it takes. Here is a suggested flow:

1. You might begin by actually reading the italicized text in the Abiding section: "Pause at the start/ end of this day. Enjoy communion with the living God . . ." Or maybe start this time by singing a song together (e.g., a song from the back of the book or one from your church's worship service).
2. Then invite some reflection on the scripture reading you just heard together by asking simple questions: "What did you hear in that passage?" "What stuck out to you?" "What did Jesus do?" "What do you think it meant when it said _____?" You might get asked a question that you don't know the answer to, and that's perfectly fine! We are all always learning together.
3. From here you could pray one of the provided prayers in the LPP for that day, you could pray using one or more of the prompts, you could pray as the passage you heard leads you, or you could practice intercessory prayer.

- THE LORD'S PRAYER: Simply pray this together every day as Jesus taught us.
- BENEDICTION (feel free to call it a "blessing" or "God's good word"): When we practice this element, the person giving the benediction raises their hands and puts them outward while the rest around the table open their hands, palms up, in a posture of reception. Then the benediction is spoken and the time of prayer comes to an end.

This is merely a suggested method, and you are encouraged to modify, reduce, or expand it as fits the context of your household. Our prayer is that you can find your communal rhythm of communing with the Creator and experience the beauty and shalom that comes from praying together.

Let us pray,
*Joel Littlepage*

## Seasons of the Christian Year

At the Daily Prayer Project we practice the global and historical tradition of the Christian year (sometimes called the liturgical year or church year) as a communal rhythm that forms us—year after year, season after season—to be the people of God and the bearers of God's story. Human beings are creatures fundamentally and profoundly shaped by stories. Each of our lives will always be following someone's calendar and bearing someone's story, but the question is: whose story is it, and what kind of narrative it is telling? The Christian year is an ancient Christian tradition of ordering the 365-day calendar year around the life of Christ. Some dates and celebrations vary by Eastern and Western Christian traditions, but they are generally as follows: Advent, Christmastide, Epiphany (also called Ordinary Time in some traditions), Lent, Eastertide, and Ordinary Time.

The Daily Prayer Project crafts each edition of the LPP in accordance with the Christian year, with six editions per annual cycle. Most editions average eight weeks, except the Pentecost and Ordinary Time editions, which span about thirteen weeks each. Christmas and Epiphany (with Epiphanytide extending through the eve of Ash Wednesday) are combined into a single edition, and we celebrate the season of Pentecost from the day of Pentecost to the eve of the fourteenth Sunday of Ordinary Time. Each season has been assigned a liturgical color and seasonal icon.

### PENTECOST | MAY 28–SEPTEMBER 2, 2023

Pentecost is the culminating feast of the season of Easter, concluding the season. Pentecost celebrates the sending of the Holy Spirit and the birth date of the church (Acts 2). The feast of Pentecost is Sunday, May 28. Ordinary Time begins Monday, May 29, and ends Saturday, December 2. This edition covers Sunday, May 28, through Saturday, September 2.

## 2022–2023 Christian Year

**ADVENT**
Nov 27–Dec 24

**CHRISTMAS & EPIPHANY**
Dec 25–Feb 21

**LENT**
Feb 22–Apr 8

**EASTER**
Apr 9–May 27

**PENTECOST**
May 28

**ORDINARY TIME**
May 29–Dec 2

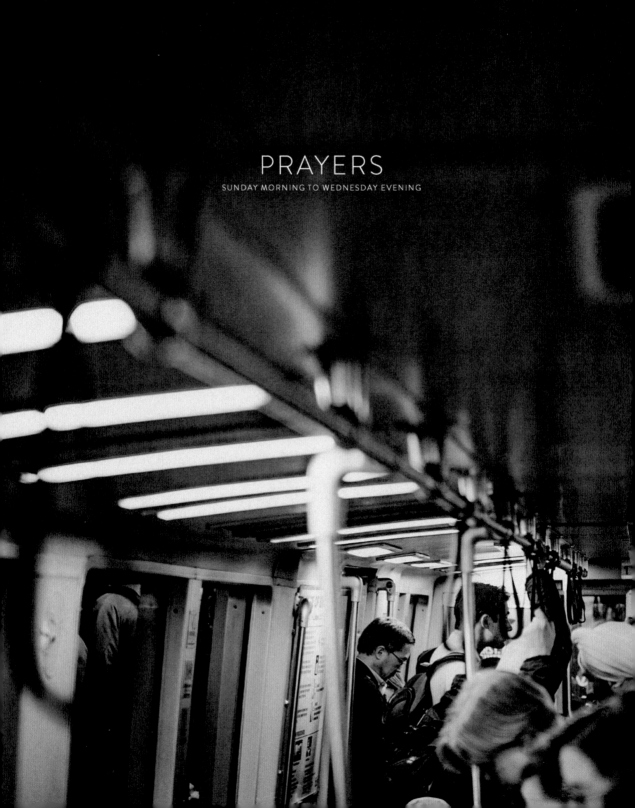

# PRAYERS

SUNDAY MORNING TO WEDNESDAY EVENING

SAN FRANCISCO
*Corey Agopian*

# SUNDAY

## Call

Let everything that has breath
praise the LORD!
**Praise the LORD!**

*Psalm 150:6*

## Psalm

*Read the Psalm of the day.*

THE GLORIA

Glory be to the Father, and to the
Son, and to the Holy Spirit;
As it was in the beginning, is now, and
ever shall be: world without end. Amen.

## Adoration

SILENCE OR SONG

*Seasonal song selections can be found on pp. 47–51.*

## Lesson

*Read the New Testament passage of the day.*

## Prayer

O Spirit of the living God,
thou light and fire divine,
descend upon thy church once more,
and make it truly thine.
Fill it with love and joy and power,
with righteousness and peace;
till Christ shall dwell in human hearts,
and sin and sorrow cease.
Blow, wind of God! With wisdom blow
until our minds are free
from mists of error, clouds of doubt,
which blind our eyes to thee.
Burn, winged fire! Inspire our lips
with flaming love and zeal,
to preach to all thy great good news,
God's glorious commonweal.

From a hymn by Henry Hallam Tweedy (1868–1953) of
America

## Abiding

LECTIO DIVINA, VISIO DIVINA, OR PRAXIO
DIVINA

*Pause at the start of a new day. Enjoy communion with the living
God: Father, Son, and Holy Spirit. Listen for the voice of God in the
scriptures. Read. Meditate. Pray. Contemplate. Seek God's face.*

PROMPTED PRAYER

- For the unified worship and witness
  of the church in every nation
- For those who are struggling
  to believe today
- For those who worship in prison

THE LORD'S PRAYER

Our Father who art in heaven, hallowed
be thy name. Thy kingdom come, thy
will be done, on earth as it is in heaven.
Give us this day our daily bread; and forgive
us our debts, as we forgive our debtors;
And lead us not into temptation,
but deliver us from evil.
For thine is the kingdom and the
power and the glory, forever. Amen.

## Benediction

Hear the Most High say: I will put my
Spirit within you, and you shall live.
May you go from this place with an
awareness of the living Spirit within you.

*Adapted from Ezekiel 37:14a*

**MAY 28**
PS. 104
NUM. 11:24-30
JOHN 20:19-23;
ACTS 2:1-21

**JUN 4**
*Trinity Sunday*
PS. 8
GEN. 1:1-2:4A
MATT. 28:16-20;
2 COR. 13:11-13

**JUN 11**
PS. 33
GEN. 12:1-9
MATT. 9:9-13, 18-26;
ROM. 4:13-25

**JUN 18**
PS. 116
GEN. 18:1-15
MATT. 9:35-10:8;
ROM. 5:1-8

**JUN 25**
PS. 86
GEN. 21:8-21
MATT. 10:24-39;
ROM. 6:1B-11

**JUL 2**
PS. 13
GEN. 22:1-14
MATT. 10:40-42;
ROM. 6:12-23

**JUL 9**
PS. 45
GEN. 24:34-67
MATT. 11:16-30;
ROM. 7:15-25

MORNING PRAYER

## Call

But I trust in you, O LORD;
I say, "You are my God."
**My times are in your hand.**

*Psalm 31:14–15a*

## Psalm

*Read the Psalm of the day.*

### THE GLORIA

Glory be to the Father, and to the
Son, and to the Holy Spirit;
As it was in the beginning, is now, and
ever shall be: world without end. Amen.

## Adoration

### SILENCE OR SONG

*Seasonal song selections can be found on pp. 47–51.*

## Lesson

*Read the Old Testament passage of the day.*

## Prayer

For your Spirit, holy God,
we pray, the Spirit
with which you equipped your prophets,
apostles, martyrs, and confessors,
the Spirit who opens our hearts for
your service as he did theirs.
We seek our neighbors, and find them only
when we open our hearts to them.
We must speak your word to them aright.
They must understand that
you are their Redeemer.
Otherwise they are lost.

Come, Holy Spirit, prepare us
to enter the huts of others.
Amen.

*A prayer of a young Ghanaian Christian,*
*taken from I Lie on My Mat and Pray*

## Abiding

### LECTIO DIVINA, VISIO DIVINA, OR PRAXIO DIVINA

*Pause at the end of this day. Enjoy communion with the living God:*
*Father, Son, and Holy Spirit. Listen for the voice of God in the*
*scriptures. Read. Meditate. Pray. Contemplate. Seek God's face.*

### INTERCESSORY PRAYER

Pray for the known needs of your
church, neighborhood, city, and world.

## Benediction

Now the Lord is the Spirit, and where the
Spirit of the Lord is, there is freedom. And
we all, with unveiled face, beholding the
glory of the Lord, are being transformed
into the same image from one degree of
glory to another. For this comes from the
Lord who is the Spirit. May you rest now
in the freedom of the Spirit of God.

*2 Corinthians 3:17–18*

**JUL 16**
PS. 45
GEN. 24:34-67
MATT. 11:16-30;
ROM. 7:15-25

**JUL 23**
PS. 119:105-112
GEN. 25:19-34
MATT. 13:1-23;
ROM. 8:1-11

**JUL 30**
PS. 128
GEN. 29:15-28
MATT. 13:31-33,
44-52;
ROM. 8:26-39

**AUG 6**
PS. 17
GEN. 32:22-31
MATT. 14:13-21;
ROM. 9:1-5

**AUG 13**
PS. 105
GEN. 37:1-28
MATT. 14:22-33;
ROM. 10:5-15

**AUG 20**
PS. 133
GEN. 45:1-15
MATT. 15:10-28;
ROM. 11:1-32

**AUG 27**
PS. 124
EXOD. 1:8-2:10
MATT. 16:13-20;
ROM. 12:1-8

EVENING PRAYER

# MONDAY

MORNING PRAYER

## Call

The Spirit of God has made me, **and the breath of the Almighty gives me life.**

*Job 33:4*

## Psalm

*Read the Psalm of the day.*

### THE GLORIA

Glory be to the Father, and to the Son, and to the Holy Spirit; As it was in the beginning, is now, and ever shall be: world without end. Amen.

## Adoration

### SILENCE OR SONG

*Seasonal song selections can be found on pp. 47–51.*

## Lesson

*Read the Old Testament passage of the day.*

## Prayer

Teach me how to live like you live. Teach me how to think like you think. Teach me how to feel like you feel. Teach me how to love like you love. Teach me how to breathe in the Spirit of life, and exhale the Spirit of life, moving always in oneness with you, my God. Be my Teacher, be my Guide, God of heaven, God of earth, God of the sun, God of the moon, God of the galaxies, God of the oceans, God of the mountains, God of the jungles, God of the snowcaps, God of the skies. Receive my prayer, receive me.

A prayer of Kari Kristina Reeves, adapted from *Canyon Road: A Book of Prayer*

## Abiding

### LECTIO DIVINA, VISIO DIVINA, OR PRAXIO DIVINA

*Pause at the start of a new day. Enjoy communion with the living God: Father, Son, and Holy Spirit. Listen for the voice of God in the scriptures. Read. Meditate. Pray. Contemplate. Seek God's face.*

### PROMPTED PRAYER

- For a dependence on the Spirit's power
- For those who work in education
- For those who are victims of war

### THE LORD'S PRAYER

Our Father who art in heaven, hallowed be thy name. Thy kingdom come, thy will be done, on earth as it is in heaven. Give us this day our daily bread; and forgive us our debts, as we forgive our debtors; And lead us not into temptation, but deliver us from evil. For thine is the kingdom and the power and the glory, forever. Amen.

## Benediction

If the Spirit of him who raised Jesus from the dead dwells in you, he who raised Christ Jesus from the dead will also give life to your mortal bodies through his Spirit who dwells in you. May the Lord fill you with hope in the surety of this promise.

*Adapted from Romans 8:11*

## Call

Cast your burden on the LORD,
and he will sustain you;
**he will never permit the
righteous to be moved.**

*Psalm 55:22*

## Psalm

*Read the Psalm of the day.*

THE GLORIA

Glory be to the Father, and to the
Son, and to the Holy Spirit;
As it was in the beginning, is now, and
ever shall be: world without end. Amen.

## Adoration

SILENCE OR SONG

*Seasonal song selections can be found on pp. 47–51.*

## Lesson

*Read the New Testament passage of the day.*

## Prayer

**Confession:** O Lord, who
has mercy upon all,
take away from me my sins,
and mercifully kindle in me
the fire of your Holy Spirit.
Take away from me the heart of stone,
and give me a heart of flesh,
a heart to love and adore you,
a heart to delight in you,
to follow and enjoy you,
for Christ's sake, Amen.

A prayer of Ambrose (339–397) of Milan, Italy

**Assurance:** I will sprinkle clean water on
you, and you shall be clean from all your
uncleannesses, and from all your idols
I will cleanse you. And I will give you
a new heart, and a new spirit I will put
within you. And I will remove the heart
of stone from your flesh and give you a
heart of flesh. And I will put my Spirit
within you, and cause you to walk in my
statutes and be careful to obey my rules.

*Ezekiel 36:25–27*

## Abiding

LECTIO DIVINA, VISIO DIVINA, OR PRAXIO
DIVINA

*Pause at the end of this day. Enjoy communion with the living God:
Father, Son, and Holy Spirit. Listen for the voice of God in the
scriptures. Read. Meditate. Pray. Contemplate. Seek God's face.*

INTERCESSORY PRAYER

Pray for the known needs of your
church, neighborhood, city, and world.

## Bendiction

After you have suffered a little while, the
God of all grace, who has called you to his
eternal glory in Christ, will himself restore,
confirm, strengthen, and establish you. May
you rest now in the gracious will of God.

*Adapted from 1 Peter 5:10*

JUL 17
PS. 26
1 SAM. 10
1 COR. 9

JUL 24
PS. 32
1 SAM. 16
1 COR. 15

JUL 31
PS. 38
1 SAM. 22
2 COR. 5

AUG 7
PS. 44
1 SAM. 28
2 COR. 11

AUG 14
PS. 50
2 SAM. 3
MARK 4

AUG 21
PS. 56
2 SAM. 9
MARK 10

AUG 28
PS. 62
2 SAM. 15
MARK 16

EVENING PRAYER

# TUESDAY

MORNING PRAYER

## Call
To you, O LORD, I lift up my soul.
**O my God, in you I trust.**
*Psalm 25:1–2*

## Psalm
*Read the Psalm of the day.*

THE GLORIA
Glory be to the Father, and to the
Son, and to the Holy Spirit;
As it was in the beginning, is now, and
ever shall be: world without end. Amen.

## Adoration
SILENCE OR SONG
*Seasonal song selections can be found on pp. 47–51.*

## Lesson
*Read the New Testament passage of the day.*

## Prayer
God, our Heavenly Father, we draw near
to you with thankful hearts because of all
your great love for us. We thank you most
of all for the gift of thy dear Son, in whom
alone we may be one. We are different
from one another in race and language, in
material things, in gifts, in opportunities,
but each of us has a human heart, knowing
joy and sorrow, pleasure and pain. We
are one in our need of your forgiveness,
your strength, your love; make us one in
our common response to you, that bound
by a common love and freed from selfish
aims, we may work for the good of all
and the advancement of your kingdom.
*A prayer of Queen Sālote Tupou III (1900–1965) of Tonga,
adapted from Oceans of Prayer*

**MAY 30**
PS. 135
PROV. 4
ACTS 1:15–26

**JUN 6**
PS. 141
PROV. 10
ACTS 6:1–7

**JUN 13**
PS. 147
PROV. 16
ACTS 9:32–43

**JUN 20**
PS. 3
PROV. 22
ACTS 13:13–41

**JUN 27**
PS. 9
PROV. 28
ACTS 16:16–40

**JUL 4**
PS. 15
RUTH 3
ACTS 20:1–35

**JUL 11**
PS. 21
1 SAM. 5
ACTS 24:1–27

## Abiding
LECTIO DIVINA, VISIO DIVINA, OR PRAXIO
DIVINA
*Pause at the start of a new day. Enjoy communion with the living
God: Father, Son, and Holy Spirit. Listen for the voice of God in the
scriptures. Read. Meditate. Pray. Contemplate. Seek God's face.*

PROMPTED PRAYER
- For humility in the presence of
  God and neighbor today
- For those who are disabled and
  those who care for them
- For the poor and for their welfare
  in your neighborhood and city

THE LORD'S PRAYER
Our Father who art in heaven, hallowed
be thy name. Thy kingdom come, thy
will be done, on earth as it is in heaven.
Give us this day our daily bread; and forgive
us our debts, as we forgive our debtors;
And lead us not into temptation,
but deliver us from evil.
For thine is the kingdom and the power and
the glory, forever. Amen.

## Benediction
May the God of hope fill you with all joy
and peace in believing, so that by the power
of the Holy Spirit you may abound in hope.
*Romans 15:13*

## Call

I long for your salvation, O LORD,
and your law is my delight.
**Let my soul live and praise you,
and let your rules help me.**

*Psalm 119:174–75*

## Psalm

*Read the Psalm of the day.*

### THE GLORIA

Glory be to the Father, and to the
Son, and to the Holy Spirit;
As it was in the beginning, is now, and
ever shall be: world without end. Amen.

## Adoration

### SILENCE OR SONG

*Seasonal song selections can be found on pp. 47–51.*

## Lesson

*Read the Old Testament passage of the day.*

## Prayer

Holy Ghost, fall down on me.
Let your Spirit fall down on me.
Create in me a new heart, oh God,
And renew a right spirit within me.
Cast me not away from thy
presence, oh God.
Take not thy Holy Spirit from me.
Holy Spirit, help me to walk right,
Talk right, live right; help me to be right.
Holy Ghost, fall down on me.
Let your Spirit fall down on me.

A prayer adapted from the song "Holy Spirit" by Kim Burrell,

an American gospel recording artist

## Abiding

### LECTIO DIVINA, VISIO DIVINA, OR PRAXIO DIVINA

*Pause at the end of this day. Enjoy communion with the living God: Father, Son, and Holy Spirit. Listen for the voice of God in the scriptures. Read. Meditate. Pray. Contemplate. Seek God's face.*

### INTERCESSORY PRAYER

Pray for the known needs of your
church, neighborhood, city, and world.

## Benediction

May the grace of our Lord Jesus Christ be
with your spirit, brothers and sisters. Amen.

*Adapted from Galatians 6:18*

**JUL 18**
PS. 27
1 SAM. 11
1 COR. 10

**JUL 25**
PS. 33
1 SAM. 17
1 COR. 16

**AUG 1**
PS. 39
1 SAM. 23
2 COR. 6

**AUG 8**
PS. 45
1 SAM. 29
2 COR. 12

**AUG 15**
PS. 51
2 SAM. 4
MARK 5

**AUG 22**
PS. 57
2 SAM. 10
MARK 11

**AUG 29**
PS. 63
2 SAM. 16
GAL. 1

EVENING PRAYER

# WEDNESDAY

MORNING PRAYER

## Call

The Spirit and the Bride say, "Come."
And let the one who hears say, "Come."
And let the one who is thirsty come;
**so that at the name of Jesus let
the one who desires take the
water of life without price.**

*Revelation 22:17*

## Psalm

*Read the Psalm of the day.*

**MAY 31**
PS. 136
PROV. 5
ACTS 2:22-47

**JUN 7**
PS. 142
PROV. 11
ACTS 6:8-7:53

**JUN 14**
PS. 148
PROV. 17
ACTS 10:1-48

**JUN 21**
PS. 4
PROV. 23
ACTS 13:42-14:7

**JUN 28**
PS. 10
PROV. 29
ACTS 17:1-15

**JUL 5**
PS. 16
RUTH 4
ACTS 20:36-21:16

**JUL 12**
PS. 22
1 SAM. 6
ACTS 25:1-22

THE GLORIA

Glory be to the Father, and to the
Son, and to the Holy Spirit;
As it was in the beginning, is now, and
ever shall be: world without end. Amen.

## Adoration

SILENCE OR SONG

*Seasonal song selections can be found on pp. 47–51.*

## Lesson

*Read the Old Testament passage of the day.*

## Prayer

**Confession:** Father, who formed the
human family to live in harmony and peace,
we acknowledge before you our divisions,
quarrels, hatreds, injustices, and greed. May
your church demonstrate before the world
the power of the gospel to destroy division,
so that, in Christ Jesus, there may be no
barriers of wealth or class, age or intellect,
race or color, but all may be equally your
children, members one of another and heirs
together of your everlasting kingdom.

A prayer of Nigerian Christians, taken from *Seeing Christ in
Others*

**Assurance:** Do you not know that your
body is a temple of the Holy Spirit within
you, whom you have from God? You are
not your own, for you were bought with
a price. So glorify God in your body.

*1 Corinthians 6:19–20*

## Abiding

LECTIO DIVINA, VISIO DIVINA, OR PRAXIO
DIVINA

*Pause at the start of a new day. Enjoy communion with the living
God: Father, Son, and Holy Spirit. Listen for the voice of God in the
scriptures. Read. Meditate. Pray. Contemplate. Seek God's face.*

PROMPTED PRAYER

- For the Lord to restore to you
  "the joy of your salvation"
- For a resistance to the idolatry
  of money, sex, and power
- For those who are married

THE LORD'S PRAYER

Our Father who art in heaven, hallowed
be thy name. Thy kingdom come, thy
will be done, on earth as it is in heaven.
Give us this day our daily bread; and forgive
us our debts, as we forgive our debtors;
And lead us not into temptation,
but deliver us from evil.
For thine is the kingdom and the power and
the glory, forever. Amen.

## Benediction

Jesus said to them again, "Peace be with
you. As the Father has sent me, even
so I am sending you." And when he
had said this, he breathed on them and
said to them, "Receive the Holy Spirit."
May the peace of Christ be with you.

*Adapted from John 20:21–22*

# WEDNESDAY

## Call

Where shall I go from your Spirit?
**Or where shall I flee from your presence?**

*Psalm 139:7*

## Psalm

*Read the Psalm of the day.*

### THE GLORIA

Glory be to the Father, and to the
Son, and to the Holy Spirit;
As it was in the beginning, is now, and
ever shall be: world without end. Amen.

## Adoration

### SILENCE OR SONG

*Seasonal song selections can be found on pp. 47–51.*

## Lesson

*Read the New Testament passage of the day.*

## Prayer

The fruit of the Spirit is
love,
joy,
peace,
patience,
kindness,
goodness,
faithfulness,
gentleness,
self-control.
Holy Spirit, please cultivate
this fruit in my life.

*Adapted from Galatians 5:22–23*

Pray through this verse slowly and repetitively.

## Abiding

LECTIO DIVINA, VISIO DIVINA, OR PRAXIO
DIVINA

*Pause at the end of this day. Enjoy communion with the living God:
Father, Son, and Holy Spirit. Listen for the voice of God in the
scriptures. Read. Meditate. Pray. Contemplate. Seek God's face.*

### PRAYER OF MINDFULNESS

*Throughout the history of the church, Christians have incorporated
practices of prayer that call to mind God's presence in the moment,
humbly and gratefully review the time that has passed, and look
forward to the gift of another day. Pray through these prompts slowly,
giving time to each step of the practice.*

1. Become aware of God's presence.
2. Review the day with gratitude.
3. Pay attention to your emotions.
4. Choose one feature of the
   day and pray from it.
5. Look toward tomorrow.

## Benediction

The LORD bless you and keep you;
the LORD make his face to shine
upon you and be gracious to you;
the LORD lift up his countenance
upon you and give you peace.

*Numbers 6:24–26*

**JUL 19**
PS. 28
1 SAM. 12
1 COR. 11

**JUL 26**
PS. 34
1 SAM. 18
2 COR. 1

**AUG 2**
PS. 40
1 SAM. 24
2 COR. 7

**AUG 9**
PS. 46
1 SAM. 30
2 COR. 13

**AUG 16**
PS. 52
2 SAM. 5
MARK 6

**AUG 23**
PS. 58
2 SAM. 11
MARK 12

**AUG 30**
PS. 64
2 SAM. 17
GAL. 2

EVENING PRAYER

PRACTICES

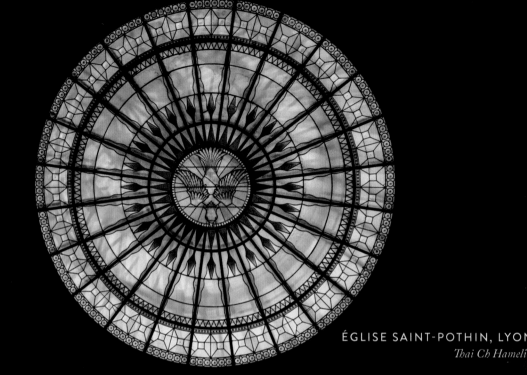

PRACTICE: SERVICE

# LIVING PENTECOSTALLY

*James Kessler*

## MEDITATION

"And suddenly there came from heaven a sound like a mighty rushing wind . . ." (Acts 2:2)

Pentecost threatens the way things are, the liturgy of life that we gather under the heading "It is what it is." A promise from the ascending Lord was that power would come upon the apostles; a *glory* would rest upon them, for the world's saving.

The late, great David Rakoff described his strategy for survival in the world as *defensive pessimism*, which involves lowering your expectations, creatively imagining the catastrophes to come and rehearsing solutions in advance. Rakoff believed that to survive in an indifferent universe, it is best to imagine its opposition to your everyday living, to protect yourself against disappointment. This is a reverse Pentecost: instead of an indwelling or a filling, it is an exasperation and a quenching. David Foster Wallace identified the same cynical trait, a disease among Christians as much as non-Christians, one that stifles the living: "Few artists dare to try to talk about ways of working toward redeeming what's wrong, because they'll look sentimental and naive to all the weary ironists. Irony's gone from liberating to enslaving." The anti-Pentecost is not a weight of glory but a weight of ironic dread, traveling the icy world on crutches, holding our breath.

Pentecost isn't optimism; it's realized hope by the indwelling of the Holy Spirit. He fills us with glory rather than dread. The people of God are gathered by that wind into a temple (Eph. 2:19–22) whose function is to image and embody hope rather than to catastrophize. Herman Bavinck describes the Spirit *as calling into being in the church the diverse virtues of faith and patience, comfort and joy!* We bear witness to one another, God's insignia burned on our chests by the fires of Pentecost. Coming now and soon is the glory of a just, merciful, loving, heavy, healing order, in which God's people demonstrate creative neighbor-love and the fires of reconciliation flare as the holy, healing breath of God fills the lungs of the exasperated among us, regathering the distanced and the pessimistic.

### EXPLORATION

Sacred imagination is burned into the soul of the Pentecost church. Let's image and embody the kingdom's presence among our worlds as they truly are. What would our streets, backyards, locker rooms, and emergency rooms look like with the mighty wind of God at work? Do we dare ask? N. T. Wright describes this activity as *wrestling* in prayer to bring the healing order of God to bear. Here are some ways to wrestle in Pentecost:

**Gather the stories of grief where God has placed you.** This may be as big as the movements that shake our culture today, or as seemingly small as the child across your street experiencing the first whisper of death from the loss of a pet, or a delivery driver being overwhelmed by a rigid work schedule that will not permit them to take bathroom breaks. Jesus was very attuned to the slightest opportunity to heal. That Pentecost rushed upon the grieving is not just a detail but the shape of the Spirit's operation in the world. We must rush upon the grieving too, eager to see the presence of the kingdom there. Our anxious culture prizes the big splash over faithfulness in small things. Have we gathered these stories of grief, big or small, and wrestled with God in pleading for healing?

**Fill the empty forms of spirituality.** Cormac McCarthy's *The Road* captures the experience of a reverse-Pentecost world. The characters fight dread with empty gestures: "Evoke the forms. Where you've nothing else, construct ceremonies out of the air and breathe upon them." Because of Pentecost, we do not construct ceremonies out of the air. We have been given the Spirit of God to fill those empty forms. This means we set our tables with a eucharistic feast, incorporating strangers and sinners. We have a baptism-like ambition to bring people in. In the Pentecost church, virtual strangers become spiritual family through baptism, while the anti-Pentecost alienates people into increasingly narrow relations. We "fill the empty forms" when we seek charity in interpreting the actions of others, when we seek forgiveness instead of distance, boldly becoming one spirit with our opponents, overturning pessimism with the winds of realized hope.

James Kessler is the planting pastor of New City Presbyterian Church in Columbus, Ohio.

# RECOVERING THE SPIRITUAL SIGNIFICANCE OF MEALS

*Abraham Cho*

## MEDITATION

The entire story of redemption can be told through the various meals recorded in scripture. I don't think this is an accident. Rather, it demonstrates the truth that God has already given to each one of us the primary technology of the mission of his kingdom. This technology in some shape or form is present in every single one of our homes, no matter how big or small: the table.

At creation, God placed Adam and Eve in a garden with an abundance of provision. God made his intention clear: to feed them and to feast with them. Sadly, in response, an appetite grew for the one thing that was not theirs to hunger for. And isn't this what sin at the root is, even in us today? Sin is the desire that cannot be and refuses to be satiated. Our appetites have been disoriented from the fall, and part of the story of redemption necessarily includes God not only saving our souls but also rebuilding a table to invite us to feast with him again. It's no wonder that at the consummation of all things, we'll find ourselves at the wedding supper of the Lamb.

This creates a paradigm for us. We are called to extend the invitation to our tables, to replicate sites of hospitality, mercy, and redemption. Scholar and essayist Elaine Scarry writes, "Beauty brings copies of itself into being." We look at the sacramental table of the Lord's Supper—the breaking of bread and the pouring of wine. The sacramental table now makes a copy of itself at our kitchen tables and beyond, to the conference tables, the boardroom tables, the council tables—those are the tables at which Christians are called to say, "If I am formed by this meal with Jesus and if this beauty makes copies of itself wherever

I go, then at every table I sit at, I am to take with me the practices of reconciliation, the practices of forgiveness, and the practices of the kingdom."

Thankfully, we aren't without a model. Through the scriptures, we can ask, "How did Jesus use his meals? Who is it that Jesus eats with?" What comes to the surface quickly is that he is often seen eating with all the "wrong" people. The patronage system in Jesus's time meant that there were wealthy and influential people who would host banquets, and the purpose of these occasions was connection and networking. If you could go, you'd find people who would be able to give generously to the work you were doing. So, it was the primary way to move up the status ladder. But here comes Jesus, and he is looking to have meals with all the wrong people, the types of people who made religious folks uncomfortable. When I first noticed this years ago, it really convicted me and made me ask, "Abe, if you were to list out all the people you had meals with within the last month, how many of those people would raise the eyebrows of the religious folks you know?" I'd invite you to ask yourself the same.

I wonder if one of the best ways to measure our growth in Christlikeness is to ask: "Is my dinner guest list looking more and more like Jesus's dinner guest list? Am I breaking bread with all the wrong people? Am I breaking bread with sinners and tax collectors? Am I using my meals to subvert all the social hierarchies of our day?" One scholar says, "Jesus does more than preach repentance to sinners; he befriends them." Do you eat with the kinds of people Jesus ate with?

We are flooded with surface-level, network-type

BULGARIA
*Stefan Vladimirov*

connections, whether it's Facebook friends or social media followers or LinkedIn connections. But this world is starved for deep friendships, the type of friendships where real questions can be asked, where we can process those things that matter most in life. The table is the site and opportunity to go deeper. And the invitation of the table before us now is this: *What would it look like if Christians were known as the people who recovered the spiritual significance of meals?*

What if we saw these moments as the place for deep encounter? What would it look like if I treated my meals as sacred time? I fear that amid our pragmatism, we have lost the spiritual significance of our meals. We have allowed them to become merely about fuel for the body, but there is opportunity for so much more. What would it look like if we treated our tables, wherever they are, as a primary technology of God's mission? In Jesus, we see this is where the kingdom of God is.

## EXPLORATION

To recover the spiritual significance of meals, consider the practice of tithing your meals. If you're eating three meals a day seven days a week, that's a total of twenty-one meals. Consider dedicating two of those meals a week to communing with someone who doesn't share your faith. These meals don't have to be a full-out banquet. They can be as simple as, "Hey, I'm going to get a salad. Want to join me?" If two meals a week feels daunting, start with one or two meals a month, and go from there.

Beauty makes copies of itself. May the welcome of the Lord's table be replicated at yours so that the beauty of what Jesus has done would create a cascade of hospitality and reconciliation in every community. And may we share our tables in assurance and expectation of the day when all our tables will find their consummation at the wedding table of the Lamb.

Abraham Cho, MDiv, ThM, serves as the senior director of training for Redeemer City to City in New York and North America. He is also the minister-in-residence at Redeemer East Harlem after previously serving for fourteen years as a pastor at Redeemer Presbyterian Church in New York City.

**Breaking Bread**
*Carol Aust, 2015*
Acrylic on canvas, 5 × 9 ft.
Oakland City Church, Oakland, California

GALLERY

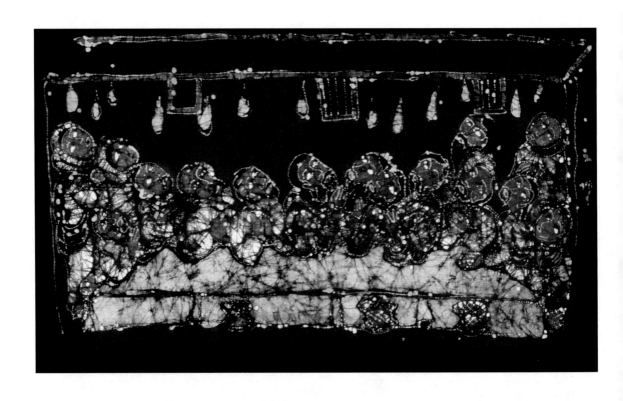

# Pentecost
*Solomon Raj*
Batik
© The Estate of P. Solomon Raj | Eyekons

# PENTECOST

Dr. P. Solomon Raj (1921–2019) was a Lutheran pastor, theologian, and artist from Andhra Pradesh, India. He worked mainly in woodcuts and batiks, a type of dyed cloth artwork made using a wax-resist method.

In this batik he shows Jesus's followers seated around a table at a house in Jerusalem when suddenly, "tongues as of fire" rush in and rest on them. They stare up in bewilderment, observing this strange phenomenon, which soon manifests itself in their newly gained ability to speak in various languages and thus to comprehensibly proclaim the gospel to the diverse crowds of Jewish pilgrims who had gathered for the festival of Pentecost, and to the many others who were present in the cosmopolitan city. This fire was the fire of Christ's Spirit, filling them with the power to be his witnesses (Acts 1:8).

Whereas in the Old Testament, the Divine Presence traveled with the Israelites by night in the form of a pillar of fire, hovering over the tabernacle whenever they set up camp, now that fire has dispersed and planted itself within all God's people, his mini-tabernacles. We bear God's presence and power. It goes with us where we go. It's partly why Jesus called his disciples "the light of the world" (Matt. 5:14). As you gaze on those golden droplets of flame in Raj's *Pentecost*, consider the gravity and the marvel that you, too, bear the flame.

# THE TRINITY

June 4 is Trinity Sunday, dedicated to celebrating the Christian mystery of the Three-in-One. Words and images can only really gesture toward, never fully explain or capture, this paradox. Still, there is value in meditating on it, as the Triune nature of God gives us a glimpse into who God is.

Consider this painting on folio 79r of a small handheld devotional book from medieval Flanders (modern-day Belgium) called the Rothschild Canticles. Most likely made for a nun, the book compiles Bible verses, liturgical praises, theological and exegetical material—and highly innovative illustrations, including a nineteen-piece sequence on the Trinity that is full of whimsy, warmth, and joy.

In this artist's conception, each person of the Trinity rides on a flaming sun, whose tentacled rays come together with the Holy Spirit as dove's tail feathers to suggest an equilateral triangle. God the Son peeks his face out from behind his fiery transport and extends an arm toward God the Father, who is completely hidden. There's a sense of dynamic energy and playfulness here! The three small suns wheel around a circle of stylized clouds and are superimposed on one large sun, symbolizing the Divine Essence. This is the *perichoresis*, or "going around," as the Greek fathers called it—the eternal dance of the Trinity. It's a relationship of coinherence and mutual love, honor, and delight.

In the four corners, heaven and earth behold the dance and rejoice. At the top, an angel or a saint hammers a row of bells with mallets, while on the ground a cloaked figure rings a handbell.

## The Trinity

*Miniature from the Rothschild Canticles,*
*probably Flanders, ca. 1300*
Beinecke Rare Book and Manuscript Library,
Yale University, New Haven, Connecticut

*View the full digitized manuscript online.*

79

## Paschal Candlestand
*Thomas Mpira, 1990*
Tangatanga wood, height 41 in.
Mua Parish Church, Malawi

# PASCHAL CANDLESTAND

Fire and wind are two symbols of the Holy Spirit— water is another. In John 7:38–39, Jesus says, "'Whoever believes in me, as the Scripture has said, out of his heart will flow rivers of living water.' Now this he said about the Spirit, whom those who believed in him were to receive." God's historic giving of the Spirit at Pentecost is described as an "outpouring." In his sermon that day, Peter quoted from the prophet Joel: "And in the last days it shall be, God declares, that I will pour out my Spirit on all flesh . . ." (Acts 2:17; cf. Joel 2:28).

In a carved Paschal candlestand by Thomas Mpira of Mua, Malawi, a river gushes forth from the Sacred Heart of the risen Christ, watering a Chewa village. His body is constituted of people who've been incorporated by his death and resurrection into the "celestial village" he holds aloft, the kingdom of God. To enter the kingdom, one must be born of water and the Spirit, Jesus tells Nicodemus (John 3:5). The newborn at the base of the stand might remind one of spiritual rebirth.

But on a literal level, this is an infant being passed over a fire, a traditional Chewa ritual that welcomes children into the community and that has been adapted by Christians in Mua for baptism liturgies.

The arched forms along the sides are stylized rainbows, symbolic of God's promise. Promise also shines forth in the candle (not pictured) that burns at the top, from amidst the thatched huts, for the duration of Eastertide and at baptisms and funerals. The candlestand is a permanent fixture at the front of Mua parish church in the diocese of Dedza.

Mpira was a regular participant in the activities of the Kungoni Centre of Culture and Art in Mua, which is still active. Founded in 1976 by Father Claude Boucher Chisale, the center employs dozens of carvers and is remarkable for how it synthesizes Christian faith and African culture.

# PRAYERS

THURSDAY MORNING TO SATURDAY EVENING

BERLIN

*Mike Kotsch*

# THURSDAY

MORNING PRAYER

**JUN 1**
PS. 137
PROV. 6
ACTS 3:1–26

**JUN 8**
PS. 143
PROV. 12
ACTS 7:54–8:3

**JUN 15**
PS. 149
PROV. 18
ACTS 11:1–18

**JUN 22**
PS. 5
PROV. 24
ACTS 14:8–28

**JUN 29**
PS. 11
PROV. 30
ACTS 17:16–34

**JUL 6**
PS. 17
1 SAM. 1
ACTS 21:17–39

**JUL 13**
PS. 23
1 SAM. 7
ACTS 25:23–26:32

## Call

Let us then with confidence draw
near to the throne of grace,
**that we may receive mercy and find
grace to help in time of need.**

*Hebrews 4:16*

## Psalm

*Read the Psalm of the day.*

### THE GLORIA

Glory be to the Father, and to the
Son, and to the Holy Spirit;
As it was in the beginning, is now, and
ever shall be: world without end. Amen.

## Adoration

### SILENCE OR SONG

*Seasonal song selections can be found on pp. 47–51.*

## Lesson

*Read the New Testament passage of the day.*

## Prayer

Rest on us,
O Spirit of Love,
and chase all anger, envy,
and bitter grudges from our souls.
Be our Comforter in trial,
when the storm goes over our heads;
be our Strength in the hour of weakness,
and help us to control the desires of the flesh.
Let us grow in faith and love,
in hope, patience, and humility.
See how many temptations surround us,
and preserve us from giving way to them;
show us the path where we should tread,
for if we trust our own impulses,
we will go astray;
but if you lead us, we shall run in the
way of your commandments.

Our hearts lie open before you;
enter now with your rich gifts,
strengthen, establish, settle them.
Dwell in them and make them your temple,
so shall we have the pledge of
the children of God,
and of our salvation.
Amen.

A prayer of Johann Friedrich Starck (1680–1756) of Germany,
adapted from *Prayers Ancient and Modern*

## Abiding

### LECTIO DIVINA, VISIO DIVINA, OR PRAXIO DIVINA

*Pause at the start of a new day. Enjoy communion with the living
God: Father, Son, and Holy Spirit. Listen for the voice of God in the
scriptures. Read. Meditate. Pray. Contemplate. Seek God's face.*

### PROMPTED PRAYER

- For patience and trust in the will of
  God in the midst of a broken world
- For social workers
- For the children who are growing
  up in your neighborhood

### THE LORD'S PRAYER

*See p. 42 for text.*

## Benediction

Humble yourselves, therefore, under
the mighty hand of God so that at the
proper time he may exalt you, casting all
your anxieties on him, because he cares
for you. May your spirit be free from
anxiety as place your life in his hands.

*1 Peter 5:6–7*

# THURSDAY

## Call

When the cares of my heart are many,
**your consolations cheer my soul.**

*Psalm 94:19*

## Psalm

*Read the Psalm of the day.*

### THE GLORIA

Glory be to the Father, and to the
Son, and to the Holy Spirit;
As it was in the beginning, is now, and
ever shall be: world without end. Amen.

## Adoration

### SILENCE OR SONG

*Seasonal song selections can be found on pp. 47–51.*

## Lesson

*Read the Old Testament passage of the day.*

## Prayer

We thank you for the benediction of
night, when the eye no longer sees,
the ear no longer hears, and the mind
no longer thinks. In that condition of
night, all humanity is completely under
your rule. Lord, let your Holy Spirit
go to work on us tonight so that when
the dawn comes, our eyes may see
aright, our ears may hear aright, and
our minds may think aright. Amen.

A prayer of an Asian Christian, adapted from *Morning, Noon and Night*

## Abiding

### LECTIO DIVINA, VISIO DIVINA, OR PRAXIO DIVINA

*Pause at the end of this day. Enjoy communion with the living God: Father, Son, and Holy Spirit. Listen for the voice of God in the scriptures. Read. Meditate. Pray. Contemplate. Seek God's face.*

### INTERCESSORY PRAYER

Pray for the known needs of your
church, neighborhood, city, and world.

## Benediction

Be still and let God's peace wash over
you like waves lapping over pebbles,
smoothing rough edges of insurmountable
worries to tiny insignificant grains of sand;
taking away the jaggedness of sin to leave
smooth, shining love. And let the peace
of God, the Father, Son and Holy Spirit,
be with us all tonight and every night.

A prayer of Lesley Steel of Scotland, adapted from *Seeing Christ in Others*

**JUL 20**
PS. 29
1 SAM. 13
1 COR. 12

**JUL 27**
PS. 35
1 SAM. 19
2 COR. 2

**AUG 3**
PS. 41
1 SAM. 25
2 COR. 8

**AUG 10**
PS. 47
1 SAM. 31
MARK 1

**AUG 17**
PS. 53
2 SAM. 6
MARK 7

**AUG 24**
PS. 59
2 SAM. 12
MARK 13

**AUG 31**
PS. 65
2 SAM. 18
GAL. 3

EVENING PRAYER

# FRIDAY

## Call

Bless the LORD, O my soul!
**O LORD my God, you are very great!**

*Psalm 104:1*

## Psalm

*Read the Psalm of the day.*

THE GLORIA

Glory be to the Father, and to the
Son, and to the Holy Spirit;
As it was in the beginning, is now, and
ever shall be: world without end. Amen.

## Adoration

SILENCE OR SONG

*Seasonal song selections can be found on pp. 47–51.*

## Lesson

*Read the Old Testament passage of the day.*

## Prayer

*No hay dios tan grande como tú,*
*no lo hay, no lo hay.*
*No hay dios que pueda hacer las obras*
*como las que haces tú.*
*No es con espada, ni con ejército,*
*mas con su Santo Espíritu.*
*Y esos montes se moverán*
*mas con su Santo Espíritú.*

There's no god as great as you,
O Lord, my God.
There's no god who works
the mighty wonders,
all the wonders that you do.
Not by our weapons, nor by our power,
but by your Holy Spirit.
And these mountains will be moved,
by your Holy Spirit.

A prayer adapted from the traditional corito "No hay dios tan grande como tú." A corito is a short praise song form used in various Latin American traditions.

## Abiding

LECTIO DIVINA, VISIO DIVINA, OR PRAXIO DIVINA

*Pause at the start of a new day. Enjoy communion with the living God: Father, Son, and Holy Spirit. Listen for the voice of God in the scriptures. Read. Meditate. Pray. Contemplate. Seek God's face.*

PROMPTED PRAYER

- For intimacy with God
- For those who work in city services
- For those who are single

THE LORD'S PRAYER

Our Father who art in heaven, hallowed
be thy name. Thy kingdom come, thy
will be done, on earth as it is in heaven.
Give us this day our daily bread; and forgive
us our debts, as we forgive our debtors;
And lead us not into temptation,
but deliver us from evil.
For thine is the kingdom and the
power and the glory, forever. Amen.

## Benediction

May the steadfast love of the Lord be
upon you even as you hope in him.

*Adapted from Psalm 33:22*

# FRIDAY

## Call

Send out your light and your truth;
let them lead me;
**let them bring me to your holy hill
and to your dwelling!**

*Psalm 43:3*

## Psalm

*Read the Psalm of the day.*

### THE GLORIA

Glory be to the Father, and to the
Son, and to the Holy Spirit;
As it was in the beginning, is now, and
ever shall be: world without end. Amen.

## Adoration

### SILENCE OR SONG

*Seasonal song selections can be found on pp. 47–51.*

## Lesson

*Read the New Testament passage of the day.*

## Prayer

In your holiness you have seen fit to make
us holy by conforming us to the image of
your Son by the work of your Spirit: and so,
in accordance with your will, we pray, Lord,
make us holy; convict us of sin; purify
our motives; cleanse our minds; wash our
hearts; strengthen our bodies and grant
us power to stand in the authority and
freedom that is abundantly and rightfully
ours as your adopted children, children of
the Living God. Grant us perseverance
and patience, cultivate within us the fruit
of the Spirit, for we groan along with all of
creation for your coming return; we wait,
together with all the saints, remembering
the plea arising continually from the
blood of the martyrs, for the day when

you will make all things new. Until that
time, sustain us and keep us in the faith,
protect us from our adversary who prowls
like a roaring lion, and put a new song in
our mouths: a song of praise to you, for
you are the same yesterday, and today, and
forever. We pray in Jesus' name, Amen.

*A prayer of Kari Kristina Reeves, adapted from Canyon Road:*
*A Book of Prayer*

## Abiding

### LECTIO DIVINA, VISIO DIVINA, OR PRAXIO
### DIVINA

*Pause at the end of this day. Enjoy communion with the living God:*
*Father, Son, and Holy Spirit. Listen for the voice of God in the*
*scriptures. Read. Meditate. Pray. Contemplate. Seek God's face.*

### INTERCESSORY PRAYER

Pray for the known needs of your
church, neighborhood, city, and world.

## Benediction

May grace be unto you and peace from
him who is and who was and who is to
come, and from the seven spirits who are
before his throne, and from Jesus Christ
the faithful witness, the firstborn of the
dead, and the ruler of kings on earth.

*Adapted from Revelation 1:4b–5*

**EVENING PRAYER**

**JUL 21**
PS. 30
1 SAM. 14
1 COR. 13

**JUL 28**
PS. 36
1 SAM. 20
2 COR. 3

**AUG 4**
PS. 42
1 SAM. 26
2 COR. 9

**AUG 11**
PS. 48
2 SAM. 1
MARK 2

**AUG 18**
PS. 54
2 SAM. 7
MARK 8

**AUG 25**
PS. 60
2 SAM. 13
MARK 14

**SEP 1**
PS. 66
2 SAM. 19
GAL. 4

# SATURDAY

## Call

Singers and dancers alike say,
**"All my springs are in you."**

*Psalm 87:7*

## Psalm

*Read the Psalm of the day.*

### THE GLORIA

Glory be to the Father, and to the
Son, and to the Holy Spirit;
As it was in the beginning, is now, and
ever shall be: world without end. Amen.

## Adoration

### SILENCE OR SONG

*Seasonal song selections can be found on pp. 47–51.*

## Lesson

*Read the New Testament passage of the day.*

### CREED

We believe in God, the Father Almighty,
Creator of the heavens and the earth;
Creator of all people and all cultures;
Creator of all tongues and races.
We believe in Jesus Christ, his Son, our Lord,
God made flesh in a person for all humanity,
God made flesh in an age for all the ages, God
made flesh in one culture for all cultures, God
made flesh in love and grace for all creation.
We believe in the Holy Spirit, through
whom God incarnate in Jesus Christ makes
his presence known in our peoples and our
cultures; through whom God, Creator of
all that exists, gives us power to become
new creatures; whose infinite gifts make
us one people: the body of Christ.
We believe in the church universal because
it is a sign of God's reign, whose faithfulness
is shown in its many hues where all the
colors paint a single landscape, where
all tongues sing the same praise.

We believe in the reign of God—the day of
the Great Fiesta when all the colors of creation
will form a harmonious rainbow, when all
peoples will join in joyful banquet, when all
tongues of the universe will sing the same song.
And because we believe, we commit
ourselves: to believe for those who do not
believe, to love for those who do not love,
to dream for those who do not dream, until
the day when hope becomes reality.

The Hispanic Creed, written by Justo L. González of Cuba.
González is a Cuban American historical theologian and
Methodist elder. Taken from *Seeing Christ in Others.*

## Prayer

O God, You are One—make us One.

A prayer from India, adapted from *Morning, Noon and Night*

## Abiding

### LECTIO DIVINA, VISIO DIVINA, OR PRAXIO DIVINA

*Pause at the start of a new day. Enjoy communion with the living
God: Father, Son, and Holy Spirit. Listen for the voice of God in the
scriptures. Read. Meditate. Pray. Contemplate. Seek God's face.*

### PROMPTED PRAYER

- For the fruit and gifts of the Holy Spirit
  to be manifested in your community
- For those who work as designers,
  writers, and artists
- For the flourishing of all people in your
  place, from the womb to the tomb

### THE LORD'S PRAYER

*See p. 42 for text.*

## Benediction

The grace of the Lord Jesus Christ and
the love of God and the fellowship
of the Holy Spirit be with you all.

*2 Corinthians 13:14*

# SATURDAY

## Call

Be merciful to me, O God,
be merciful to me,
**for in you my soul takes refuge.**

*Psalm 57:1*

## Psalm

*Read again the Psalm of the day.*

THE GLORIA

Glory be to the Father, and to the Son,
and to the Holy Spirit;
As it was in the beginning, is now, and
ever shall be: world without end. Amen.

## Adoration

SILENCE OR SONG

*Seasonal song selections can be found on pp. 47–51.*

## Lesson

*Read the Old Testament passage of the day.*

## Prayer

**Confession:** Lamb of God, you take away
the sins of the world, have mercy on us.
Lamb of God, you take away the sins
of the world, have mercy on us.
Lamb of God, you take away the sins
of the world, grant us peace.

*The Agnus Dei*

**Assurance:** Christ, our Passover lamb, has
been sacrificed. Let us therefore celebrate
the festival, not with the old leaven, the
leaven of malice and evil, but with the
unleavened bread of sincerity and truth.

*1 Corinthians 5:7–8*

## Abiding

LECTIO DIVINA, VISIO DIVINA, OR PRAXIO
DIVINA

*Pause at the end of this day. Enjoy communion with the living God:
Father, Son, and Holy Spirit. Listen for the voice of God in the
scriptures. Read. Meditate. Pray. Contemplate. Seek God's face.*

PRAYER OF MINDFULNESS

1. Become aware of God's presence.
2. Review this past week with gratitude.
3. Pay attention to your emotions.
4. Choose one feature of the
   week and pray from it.
5. Look toward tomorrow and the
   beginning of a new week.

A PRAYER FOR SABBATH

Creator God,
On the seventh day you rested
and were refreshed.
Please help me now to enter into
the rest of your Sabbath,
That I may cease from my work
And delight in your care over my life
Both now and forever,
Amen.

## Benediction

Lord, you now have set your servants free
to go in peace as you have promised, for
these eyes of ours have seen the savior,
whom you have prepared for all the world
to see: a light to enlighten the nations,
and the glory of your people Israel. Glory
to the Father, and to the Son, and to the
Holy Spirit: as it was in the beginning,
is now, and will be forever. Amen.

*The Nunc Dimittis (Song of Simeon), based on Luke 2:29–32*

EVENING PRAYER

BELARUS
*Darya Tryfanava*

SONGBOOK

# NO HAY DIOS TAN GRANDE COMO TÚ

There's no god as great as you,
O Lord, my God.
There's no god as great as you,
O Lord, my God.
There's no god who works the mighty wonders,
all the wonders that you do.
There's no god who works the mighty wonders,
all the wonders that you do.

Not by our weapons, nor by our power,
but by your Spirit we are led.
Not by our weapons, nor by our power,
but by your Spirit we are led.
And these mountains will be moved,
And these mountains will be moved,
And these mountains will be moved,
by your Holy Spirit.

Traditional Latin American corito

# REVIVE US AGAIN

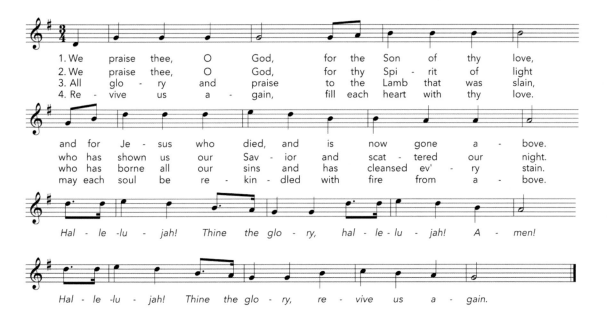

1. We praise thee, O God, for the Son of thy love,
2. We praise thee, O God, for thy Spi - rit of light
3. All glo - ry and praise to the Lamb that was slain,
4. Re - vive us a - gain, fill each heart with thy love.

and for Je - sus who died, and is now gone a - bove.
who has shown us our Sav - ior and scat - tered our night.
who has borne all our sins and has cleansed ev' - ry stain.
may each soul be re - kin - dled with fire from a - bove.

Hal - le -lu - jah! Thine the glo - ry, hal - le -lu - jah! A - men!

Hal - le -lu - jah! Thine the glo - ry, re - vive us a - gain.

Text: William Paton Mackay (1839–1885) of Scotland. Music: John H. Husband (1760–1825) of England. Public Domain.

# TRINITY SONG

Ho - ly Fath - er, Son, and Spi - rit.

Ho - ly Com - mu - nion, Three - in - One.

Come with Your peace, with Your in - vi - ta - tion.

Bind us to - ge - ther in ho - ly love.

Text and music by Sandra McCracken. ©2016 DRINK YOUR TEA MUSIC (ASCAP), admin. Music Services. All rights reserved. Used with permission.

# 오소서 (OSOSÔ)
# COME NOW, O PRINCE OF PEACE

1. O - so - so— o - so - so, pyong - hwa eui im - gum
*Come now, O— Prince of peace, make us one bod - y,*

2. O - so - so— o - so - so, sa - rang eui im - gum
*Come now, O— God of love, make us one bo - dy,*

3. O - so - so— o - so - so, cha - yu eui im - gum
*Come now, and set us free, O God, our Sav - ior,*

4. O - so - so— o - so - so, tong - il eui im - gum
*Come, Hope of— u - ni - ty, make us one bod - y,*

u - ri - ga— han - mom i - ru - ge ha - so - so.
*come, O Lord Je - sus, re - con - cile your— peo - ple.*

u - ri - ga— han - mom i - ru - ge ha - so - so.
*come, O Lord— Je - sus, re - con - cile your— peo - ple.*

u - ri - ga— han - mom i - ru - ge ha - so - so.
*come, O Lord— Je - sus, re - con - cile all— na - tions.*

u - ri - ga— han - mom i - ru - ge ha - so - so.
*come, O Lord— Je - sus, re - con - cile all— na - tions.*

1. 오소서 오소서
   평화의 임금
   우리가 한몸
   이루게 하소서

2. 오소서 오소서
   사랑의 임금
   우리가 한몸
   이루게 하소서

3. 오소서 오소서
   자유의 임금
   우리가 한몸
   이루게 하소서

4. 오소서 오소서
   통일의 임금
   우리가 한몸
   이루게 하소서

Text and music by Kǒn-yong Yi (Geon-yong Lee) (이건용) of Korea. ©1990 Geon-yong Lee. English text ©1990 Marion Pope. Arrangement ©2011 GIA Publications, Inc.

Made in the USA
Monee, IL
11 May 2023

32909807R00031